Helping in Rabbit's Garden
Table of Contents

Name: _____

Rabbit had worked hard in his garden all during the Spring. He did many things to keep his garden growing.

• First, Rabbit planted the seeds.

• Then, he watered the plants.

• After a while, the plants grew.

 Have an adult help you cut out the pictures of Rabbit in his garden. Glue them on page 3 in the correct order.

© Disney   © Disney   © Disney

Name: _____

But now, Rabbit was worried about his garden. There had been no rain in the Hundred-Acre Wood for many days.

 Draw what Rabbit needs for his garden.

As Rabbit worried, Pooh came by.
"Hello, Rabbit," said Pooh. "Isn't it a lovely day?"
"No, no, no!" said Rabbit, stomping his foot. "It's not a bit lovely!"

Name: _____

Rabbit continued, "Without rain, no garden can grow. How will I get water for my plants?"

Pooh said, "Perhaps we should think about that. Think-think."

 What can Rabbit use? Color each thing below that holds water.

5

"Perhaps we could get water from the stream with buckets," said Pooh.

"Hmm, not a bad idea," said Rabbit. "Let's go there for water."

Help Pooh and Rabbit get to the stream. Trace the *w* path.

What letter did you make by following the path? _____

6

Name: _____

After filling their buckets at the stream, Pooh and Rabbit returned to the garden. On the way, Pooh spilled all the water out of his bucket.

"Now, look what you've done!" cried Rabbit. "I'll get water on my own, Pooh."

 Circle the things that are full. Cross out the things that are empty.

"Oh, bother," Pooh said. "If I can't carry water, how can I help?" He decided to visit Piglet for an answer.

Name: _____

Pooh told Piglet about Rabbit's dry garden.
"Why don't we try a rain song?" said Piglet.
"I don't know any rain songs," said Pooh. "Do you?"
Piglet said, "Well, no. P-P-Perhaps we can make one up."

Help Pooh and Piglet with their rain song. Circle the picture that completes each rhyme on page 9.

Name: _____

Dear Mr. Rain Cloud,

The ground is quite dry.

We need lots of rain

To fall from the .

sky   clouds

Dear fluffy rain cloud,

Our message is plain–

Open up wide

And send us some .

snow   rain

No rain came. Pooh and Piglet waited and waited. Still no rain.
"Piglet, I don't think the clouds heard us," said Pooh.
"Then, let's ask everyone else to come and help," said Piglet.
"Christopher Robin can help us write a note."

Name: _____

 Use the pictures to read Pooh and Piglet's note below.

Name: _____

All the friends in the Hundred-Acre Wood wanted to help Rabbit. They all went to the stream. They had buckets for carrying the water to the garden. Everyone had a bucket just the right size for himself.

 Draw a line to match each friend to the correct size of bucket.

 Name: _____

Tigger said, "Look at me! I'm usin' my smarts and carryin' two buckets of water. You fellas should all do it the tiggery way."

 Draw another bucket for Pooh so he has **2** buckets.

 Trace the number **2**. Then, write it on your own.

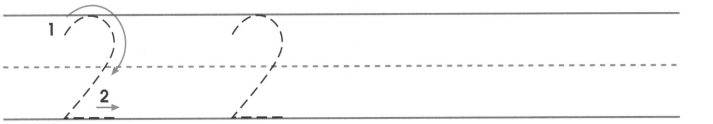

13

Name: _____

Suddenly, Owl said, "Well, I say now! Perhaps there's a way we could carry even more buckets! Pooh, may we use your wagon? It would hold even more than two."

 Kanga loaded the big buckets into Pooh's wagon. Roo loaded the small buckets into the wagon. Count the buckets below and write each answer on page 15.

Name: _____

• How many blue buckets are there? _____

• How many red buckets are there? _____

• How many small red buckets are there? _____

• How many buckets are there altogether? _____

Even with many buckets of water, Rabbit's garden was still dry.

"It all comes from having a garden that's too big!" said Rabbit. "Now, what will I do?"

Name: _____

Kanga asked, "Gopher, dear, perhaps you could make a tunnel from the stream to the garden! Then, lots of water could get here." Gopher said, "I'll get s-s-started right now!"

 Help Gopher make his tunnel. Follow the directions below to trace his path on page 17.

• Gopher started digging at the garden. He tunneled down.

• Gopher tunneled right and down past the root.

• Gopher tunneled under the rock.

• Gopher tunneled up to the left of the ants.

• Gopher tunneled right to the stream.

Way to go!

Nice job!

Just lovely!

Lookin' good, little buddy!

A-ma-zing!

You're on top!

Tigger-ific!

P is for perfect!

Excellent!

Hoo-hoo-hoo!

Hoo–hoo–hoo!
We're happy for you!

Good for you!

A honey of a job!

Well done!

Funtastic!

Kickerific

Hip–hip–hooray!

Splendiferous!

Good think–think–thinking!

Marvelous!

Name: _____

As Gopher finished his tunnel, everyone heard the water rush in. But no water came out. Gopher looked down into his hole. "S-S-Say! My tunnel has turned to mud!" said Gopher. "This won't work."

Name: _____

Rabbit said, "Oh, dear! Oh, dear! I do wish we could make the stream come to *us*."

"Splendid idea, Rabbit!" said Owl. "We'll *make* something to help the water come to us. Here's what we'll need."

 Write the beginning sound for each thing Rabbit and his friends need.

_____ope

_____ox

_____ire

_____ail

Name: _____

Piglet asked, "But where will we get these things?"
"You just leave that to me!" said Tigger. "I'll getcha that stuff."

 Help Tigger find what he needs. Circle the picture that has the same shape as the picture in the box.

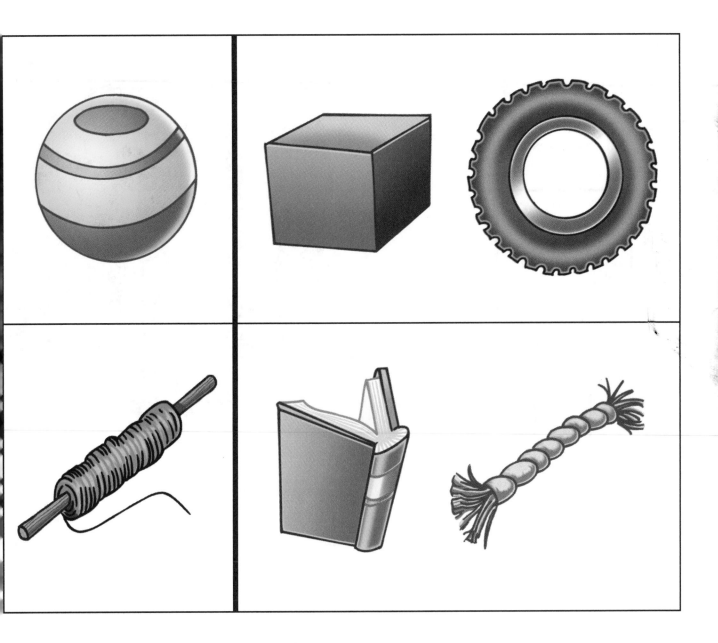

Name: _____

After Tigger had found everything they needed, Rabbit, Owl, and their friends put a Stream-Moving Machine together.

 Help make the machine. Have an adult help you cut out the shapes on the left. Glue each shape in the place that matches it.

20

Name: _____

Name: _____

"How will this machine help my garden?" asked Rabbit.
"Well, now," Owl replied, "Allow me to show you."

 Help Owl show how the machine moves. Trace the dotted lines with a pencil.

22

Name: _____

Owl explained, "To begin, one must hang buckets full of water on the rope. Then, the rope goes around this way. The buckets move from the stream to Rabbit's house."

Name: _____

Pooh asked, "Then, how do we get the water to the garden?"
Owl said, "Yes, yes, yes, yes. Obviously, we thought of that part, too!"

"First, take the full bucket off the hanger.

Second, pour the water onto the plant.

Third, put the empty bucket back on the hanger."

 Show how to get water to the garden. Number the pictures below in order.

24

Name: _____ © _____

Everyone got into place. They started the machine.
"It works!" cried Rabbit. "Ha-ha! We did it!"
So, Rabbit's friends came every day to water his garden.

 What do you think happened next in Rabbit's garden? Color the picture that shows it.

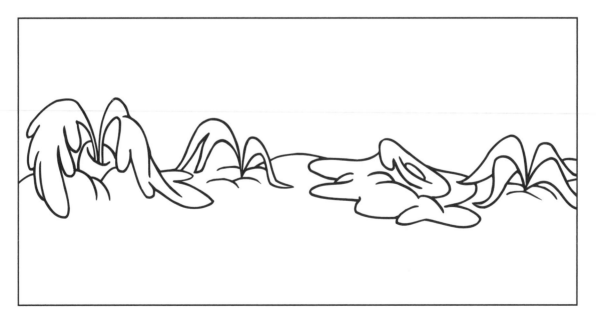

25

Name: _____

And Rabbit's plants grew larger and better than ever.

 Have an adult help you cut out the pictures. Glue them in place below and on page 27 to complete the patterns.

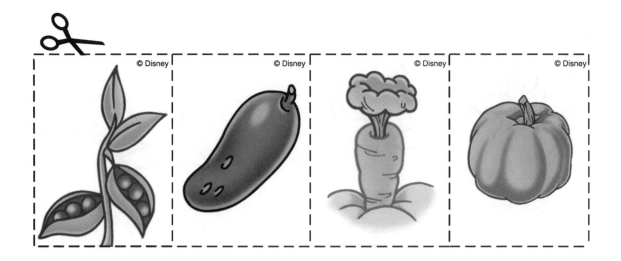

© Disney   © Disney   © Disney   © Disney

Name: _____

Finally, it was time to pick the vegetables. Rabbit had a picnic and invited everyone to eat all the good things from his garden.

 Read the clues. Have an adult help you cut out each picture. Glue the pictures in the places where they belong on page 29.

- The one who ate a carrot sat between Piglet and Owl.

- Eeyore did not eat corn.

- Tigger ate something yellow.

© Disney © Disney © Disney

Name: _____

Rabbit made a speech. "Well, well, well. It seems that you all have helped to save my garden. I hope you enjoy this vegetable feast as my way of saying thank you."

"We will!" Roo cried.

"Did I just feel a raindrop?" asked Pooh.

Helping Your Child at Home

Mathematics Readiness

Helping your preschool or kindergarten child develop mathematics concepts and readiness skills is critical to his/her success in mathematics. **Mathematics readiness skills** include counting and gaining an understanding of how numbers are used in the world around us. The activities in this book and those suggested below are ways you can help your child develop these skills at home.

Go on a "number hunt" around the house. Help your child find numbers on the television, VCR, clock, telephone, oven, calendar, etc. Talk about how the numbers are used on each.

Give your child a set of dominoes and let him/her explore with them. Have your child count the number of dots and match the sides that have the same number of dots. Your child can also build with the dominoes and count how many pieces he/she uses.

Help your child sort candies into color groups and count the number of candies in each group. Then, ask him/her: Which group has the most? The fewest? Which groups have the same number?

Read number books with your child, such as *Roll Over: A Counting Song* by Merle Peek or *Ten Sly Piranhas* by William Wise. Teach your child number rhymes and songs, such as "One, Two, Buckle My Shoe," "This Old Man," or "Over in the Meadow."

Page 3.

Page 4.

Answer will vary,
but should show
rain or water.

Page 5.

Page 6.

What letter did you make by following the path? ___W___

Page 7.

Page 9.

sky   clouds

snow   rain

Page 11.

Dear Friends,
   Rabbit needs help.
Go to his garden.
He needs water.
        From,
   Pooh and Piglet

Page 12.

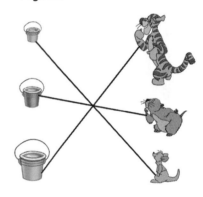

Page 13.

Page 15.

How many blue buckets are there?	4
How many red buckets are there?	3
How many small red buckets are there?	2
How many buckets are there altogether?	7

Page 17.

Page 18.

Page 19.

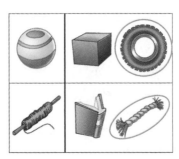

Page 20-21.

Page 24.

Page 25.

Page 26.

Page 27.

Page 29.